United States First Women

A Look into the Lives and Legacy of 5 Influential American First Ladies

By Naven Johnson

Table of Contents

History of Women's Rights 4

Abigail Adams...10

Dolley Madison 14

Eleanor Roosevelt 18

National Youth Administration...21

Civil Rights Activism 23

Hillary Clinton...27

Michelle Obama 34

History of Women's Rights

Women didn't always have the rights and the possibilities that they do today. In the past, the basic human rights such as: the right to vote, the right to reproduce, the right to work, to hold public office, to enter into legal contracts, to have equal rights in family law, the right to education, the right to be free from sexual violence, the right to own property and so on, were not available to women.

The word "feminism" first appeared in 1872 in the Netherlands and France, in the 1890s in Britain, and in 1910 in the U.S. Depending on the time, this word meant various things, and the feminists around the world had different causes and goals that they wanted to achieve with this movement. The history of feminism can be observed in three waves and each of those waves addressed different issues and problems that women had.

The first wave of feminism took place in the 19th and early 20th century. During this period, the US and UK promoted equal contract, marriage, parenting and property rights for women. The second wave began in the mid-twentieth century. In that time most of the countries in Europe still didn't provide satisfactory rights for women. Women fought for the right to vote all over Europe. In this period, women fought for the abolition of the "marital exemption" in rape laws which disallowed the prosecution of husbands for the rape of their wives. The third wave took place in the late twentieth and early twenty-first centuries. Third-wave feminism distinguished itself from the second wave around matters of sexuality, challenging female heterosexuality and celebrating sexuality as a means of female empowerment.

During the last decades, there were those who still believed that women lacked the intellectual capacity to be leaders and make important business decisions. They weren't biased they just thought that women didn't have the right emotional endurance because of their biology. As time passes by, these opinions are slowly but surely changing. Even though in a lot of places in the world women are still oppressed and are believed to be intellectually incapable of being anything more than a spouse and a mother, most of the countries in the world are making progress when it comes to the overall rights of women. This is apparently a result of businesses being more profitable, governments more representative, and communities healthier.

The fact that women are different than men is totally true. By experiencing things differently, they think about problems and solutions differently too. And as we all know, diversity is always an asset. With diversity you can analyze problems differently, you can look at the world and the problems that the world is facing differently. This will result in offering different solutions to the same problems. The diversity itself broadens the horizon and enriches the process of thinking.

The fact that women and men are different is actually a good thing. Women lead differently than men, they are more likely to collaborate with others, to be team-oriented. These characteristics are crucial in today's innovation-driven world. Women are less likely to get in conflicts also. The former president of Ireland, Mary Robinson, thinks that women bring inter-generational perspective into their work. They are more likely to think about the future generations when they think about what kind of decisions they are making. She thinks that women will make a safer world for their children and their grandchildren and that they will incorporate this into their leadership style.

Initially, women were expected to think more like men and to behave like them too. But pointing and accepting the differences between the sexes is very crucial for success. These differences should be observed as assets and strengths rather than weaknesses that need to be overcome. However, a lot of studies over the years show that women's efforts are less valued and they have less margin for error. Sometimes even women do this to themselves because they are afraid to take risks, to ask for promotions or ask for money. In conclusion, the benefits of empowering women are huge and they can't be denied.

Women are the engine driving global economic growth. By 2014, women were responsible for approximately $28tn. Along the other differences in thinking, and analyzing, women also spend their money differently. They tend to put their families and children first and raise them in better conditions. They invest in healthier food, better schools, improving healthcare and education. They start businesses and they give jobs to other women which results in prosperity for the whole community.

For these reasons, investing in women has been increasing over the years and it has become a strategic imperative for a lot of companies worldwide. It is important to mention that women are essential to building and nourishing peace. It is believed that women help decrease the gap between different groups. Because of women, a lot of different problems are addressed in the companies such as sexual violence, food security and so on. All of this results in more peaceful working places.

Former US Secretary of State Dr. Condoleezza Rice made a statement that supports this. She said that women are guardians in different spheres of life, that they carry the biggest load on their shoulders and that they can help humanity heal. We need to be aware that empowering women is not only about being politically correct, but it is about improving overall outcomes in our companies and societies.

Abigail Adams

The second President of the United States was John Adams who was inaugurated on March 4th, 1797 in Philadelphia. At the moment of the inauguration, Abigail was tending to her dying mother. After her husband was elected President, she held glamorous large dinners every week, she made a lot of public appearances and was in charge of the city entertainment for each Fourth of July in the city of Philadelphia. Her role was being active in politics and she was completely different than Martha Washington who was quiet for most of her husband's career.

Abigail was so politically involved that her political opponents referred to her as "Mrs. President". She worked as John's confidant and because of that she was always informed about issues that were in her husband's administration. She often included a lot of details that were not known to the public in letters that she addressed to her sister Mary and nephew John Quincy. Abigail was being used by a lot of people who wanted to get in touch with the President himself. She was supportive of her husband and his policies and she often gave stories about him to the press.

Adams soon became the first lady to live in the White House after the relocation of the capital city in 1800 to Washington D.C. They moved there in November and lived there for only four months before John's term ended. At that time the city was a wilderness and the White House was far from being finished but Abigail liked it and thought it was very beautiful. The only complaint she had is that nobody was willing to chop wood for the necessities of the White House even though the house was surrounded by nature.

Abigail spoke out about women's rights as an 18th-century woman. She was aware that a lot of women in that period of time were oppressed by their husbands, families and the societies they lived in. She was an advocate for the rights of married women, especially in the area of property rights and education opportunities. Her belief was that women should not be satisfied with laws that do not meet their needs and that they should reach for more than just being men's companions.

She put education on top of her fights for women's rights because she thought that women should be considered as intellectually capable of educating themselves and raising their children better. In March 1776, she sent a letter to John and the Continental Congress in which she requested that women should be treated better than they were. She wrote that husbands should not have unlimited power over women and she announced that she was willing to form a Rebellion in order to fight for women's rights. She also pointed out that women would not be bound by any laws that do not represent women's rights as they should.

Abigail didn't agree with slavery either. She believed that it was evil and inhumane and she considered it to be a threat to the American democratic society. On 31 March 1776, she wrote a letter in regards to slavery in which she pointed out that she doubts that most of the people who had a passion for liberty are true to themselves because they are depriving their fellow humans of such rights.

In 1791 a free black boy came to her house and asked if he could be taught how to read and write. She granted his request and put the boy into an evening school even beside the fact that the neighbors complained. Her beliefs were that the boy should not be denied the ability to earn a livelihood in the future by working on himself just because of the color of his skin. After the end of John's term he tried to get re-elected but was not successful and the family retired to Quincy in 1800. Adams supported her son during his political career, she lost her daughter to breast cancer and she raised her grandchildren. She passed away in the 73rd year of her life on October 28th, 1818.

Dolley Madison

Dolley Madison was the wife of the President of the United States (James Madison) from 1809 to 1817. She was recognized for her social graces that brought a lot of fame to her husband. Dolley used to serve this role later known as First Lady for the widower Thomas Jefferson. She accompanied him for official ceremonial functions.

The architect Benjamin Henry Latrobe worked on the White House and Dolley helped him to furnish it fully. In 1808, Thomas Jefferson was ready to retire, and the Democratic-Republican caucus nominated James Madison and he was elected President. James Maddison served two terms and Dolley became the first official First Lady. Dolly was also the first First Lady and first American to respond to a telegraph message. She was also granted the honorary seat on the floor of Congress.

In 1812, the War of 1812 began with Great Britain. That same year the United States declared war on Canada and the next year tried to invade the country. As the situation escalated, all the staff from the White House prepared to leave. Dolley ordered that the Stuard painting be removed. The painting was a copy of the famous Lansdowne portrait. The picture was secured and it required to be unscrewed from the wall.

In those moments, that was too much to ask from the staff so she ordered the staff to break the frame and to take out the canvas only. The canvas was placed in a safe place in New York. After the war, Dolly was given the credit for taking down the painting and she became a national heroine even though the house slaves were the ones that actually preserved the painting. Dolley along with the family fled the city and went to Virginia. After the danger was gone she returned in Washington to her husband.

Montpelier and Washington

After James Madison retired in 1817, he and his wife Dolley returned to Montpelier plantation in Orange County. A few years later, their son Payne Todd who never found a career went to prison and they had to mortgage the plantation to pay off his debts. In 1836 James Madison passed away and Dolley stayed on the plantation for one more year before returning back to Washington. She left Todd in charge of the plantation and took her niece Anna with her to Washington.

Todd couldn't take proper care of the plantation while his mother was in the city due to severe alcoholism and illnesses related to his addiction. Dolley tried to raise money by selling some properties of her husband and her butler, but couldn't raise enough. She sold Montpelier along with the furnishings and the slaves. Her butler Paul

Jennings later explained in his memoirs that in the last days of her life, Dolley struggled financially even with the main necessities for living. Paul often visited her and would always bring her food and other things he thought she needed. She died at her home in Washington in 1849 at the age of 81.

Eleanor Roosevelt

Eleanor Roosevelt was Franklin D. Roosevelt's wife. She became the First Lady of the United States on March 4th, 1933. She was aware of the part that the previous First Ladies played in the careers of their husbands and she was really depressed because of it. The role that they played was traditionally limited to being a hostess for events and being just a figure next to the President. Eleanor was seriously distressed at these standards, so she set up to redefine the role of the First Lady.

Later, her biographer Cook named her to be the most controversial First Lady in United States history. Her husband, the President supported her and with his support she began to develop a career as a First Lady in a time where not many married women had careers at all. She was the first presidential spouse that regularly held press conferences and she became the first to speak at a national party convention in 1940. She wrote a daily newspaper column "My Day" as well. She hosted a weekly radio show. All of these things were first started by her. During the first year of Franklin's administration, his wife was determined to earn as much as the presidential salary. She earned a lot from her writing and lectures and most of those funds she gave away to charity. She worked very hard in her twelve years in the White House and she was making numerous personal appearances at labor meetings.

In 1932, a protest group of World War I veterans marched on Washington making demands about their veteran bonus certificates. President Herbert Hoover ordered the US Army to disperse the crowd, and they used tear gas to bombard the veterans. In 1933, they made the same protest but this year Eleanor Roosevelt made a visit to their muddy campsite and listened to their concerns and demands. As a result, the tension between the veterans and the administration defused and one veteran commented that Hoover sent the Army, and Roosevelt sent his wife.

After her husband became President, a rose was discovered and named in her honor Mrs. Franklin D. Roosevelt. It was a hybrid tea rose. In 1937 she started to work on her autobiography, and later all the volumes were combined into The autobiography of Eleanor Roosevelt in 1961.

National Youth Administration

In 1935, the American Youth Congress was formed to fight for youth rights in the United States politics. The AYC was responsible for presenting the American Youth Bill of Rights to the U.S Congress. The relationship that Roosevelt had with the AYC lead to the creation of the National Youth Administration which was a New York agency in the United States. This agency concentrated on providing education and work for American citizens between the ages of 16 and 25. The head of the NYA was Aubrey Willis Williams who was a liberal from Alabama and was also in a close relationship with Roosevelt.

Eleanor expressed her concern about the young people in the country and her fear of losing them and their potential. She thought that they should make the youth of America feel like they are needed and to incorporate them into the active life of the community. In 1939 the leaders of the AYC were subpoenaed by the Dies Committee. Roosevelt was at the hearings and afterward invited the subpoenaed witnesses to the White House. The NYA was shut down in 1943.

Civil Rights Activism

During the era of segregation, Eleanor Roosevelt became an important connection to the African-American population in the time of her husband's administration. She was very vocal in her support of the civil rights movement of the African-Americans. She was aware that the African-Americans were discriminated in every sphere, so she became the only voice in the White House who insisted on providing equal benefits for all of the American citizens no matter the race.

She would often invite African-Americans to the White House. There was an incident in 1939 involving the black singer Marian Anderson who was denied to use the Washington's Constitution Hall by the Daughters of the American Revolution. As a sign of disapproval, Eleanor resigned from the group and she helped arrange a new concert for Marian Anderson. He later performed in the White House at a dinner with the King and Queen of the United Kingdom. She was also a close friend with the African-American educator Mary McLeod Bethune who was the director of the Division of Negro Affairs in the NYA. In order to avoid any problems, Eleanor would wait for Mary at the gates of the White House and she would embrace her and bring her in arm-in-arm

Eleanor was involved in the New Deal which was a series of programs that were in response to the Great Depression. The programs focused on relief, recovery, and reform; relief for the unemployed and poor, recovery of the economy and reform of the financial system to prevent such an event from happening again. She was the eyes and ears within the New Deal. She was dedicated to the social reforms and thought about the future. One of those programs was formed in order to help women receive better working wages and to place them into less machine work and more office work. Women mostly worked in factories making war supplies in order to contribute to the war efforts.

As opposed to Eleanor's efforts to support the African-Americans, she had a sundown town named after her in West Virginia in 1934. She visited the site with her husband and developed it as a test site for people. Franklin Roosevelt had a lot of sundown towns such as Greenhills, Greendale, Greenbelt, Norris, Hanford, and these towns were only for white people. This town was recognized as one of the projects of New Deal. Eleanor also lobbied to make lynching a federal crime.

Because of the continuous support that Eleanor Roosevelt offered to the African-Americans and their civil rights, she became unpopular among the white people in the South. There were rumors that the servants formed Eleanor's Clubs with the main goal to oppose their employers. Of course, there was never any proof to support this. In 1943, a race riot broke out in Detroit and the critics blamed Roosevelt. At the same time, her popularity among the African-American people significantly grew and they became consistent supporters for the Democratic Party.

After the Japanese attack on Pearl Harbor on December 7th, 1941, Eleanor raised her voice against Japanese-American prejudice. She was very condemned for her defense of Japanese-American citizens.

Hillary Clinton

Hilary Clinton became the First Lady in 1993 when Bill Clinton took office as President of the United States. Hilary was the first First lady in the history of the United States that had her own professional career and a postgraduate degree before she was named First Lady. She was also the first to have an office in the West Wing of the White House beside the usual first lady offices in the East Wing. Hilary Clinton was said to be the most openly empowered presidential wife after Eleanor Roosevelt.

She was so empowered that even some of the critics thought that it was not appropriate for a first lady to play such a central role in matters of public policy. Her supporters responded that it was very clear about what her role would be from the very beginning. The fact that

Clinton played such an active role in her husband's presidency made opponents to refer to the Clintons as co-presidents and label them as "Billary". Hillary was also a part of a prayer group of the Fellowship, especially after her father's death.

In January 1993, Hilary was named to chair a Task Force on National Health Care Reform by her husband. He hoped that they could repeat the success that Hilary had with the Arkansas education reform. The recommendation of the task force became recognized as the Clinton Health Care plan which was a well-thought plan that would involve employers to provide health coverage to their employees through individual health maintenance organizations.

There were a lot of people that opposed to this plan and they announced violent protests against it so Clinton had to wear a bulletproof vest during the bus tour to rally support for the plan in 1994. The proposal failed in September 1994 because they couldn't gather enough supporters. Hilary's approval ratings fell down to 44 percent in April and 35 percent in September. Before this, her ratings were above 50 percent. This campaign was a big issue in the 1994 midterm elections.

Later in 1997, Clinton was a force behind the passage of the State Children's Health Insurance Program that gave support to children whose parents could not provide health coverage. She promoted immunization against children with diseases and encouraged women to get mammograms for free. Hilary also increased research funding for prostate cancer and childhood asthma. Clinton helped in the creation of the Office on Violence Against Women at the Department of Justice together with Attorney General Janet Reno. In the same year, 1997, she initiated the Adoption and Safe Families Act which she thought was the greatest accomplishment that she had as a first lady.

She was involved in the passage of the Foster Care Independence Act that helped teenagers aging out of foster care. Her involvement in children's welfare continued. She often hosted different White House conferences among which are the ones on Child Care in 1997, Early Childhood Development and Learning in 1997 and Children and Adolescents in 2000. She hosted many more of these conferences and during this period of time, she traveled to 79 countries. With that, she became the most traveled first lady taking the first place from Pat Nixon. Hilary played a role in U.S diplomacy even though she did not have an official clearance or attendance at the National Security Council meetings. One of her five-nation trips to South Asia in 1995 sought to improve relations with India and Pakistan. This trip was the beginning of her eventual career in diplomacy.

In a speech that Clinton made in 1995 just before the Fourth Women Conference on Women in Beijing, she spoke out against abuse towards women in the world and in China itself. She said that it is no longer acceptable to treat woman's rights as anything different than simple human rights. Her speech was heard from delegates from over 180 countries and it became a key moment in the empowerment of women. Women around the world would recite her words years later.

Hilary's Traditional Duties

When it comes to the traditional duties that Hilary had as a First Lady, she did a great job too. Clinton placed donated handicrafts of modern American artisans inside the White House such as glassware and pottery. She oversaw the restoration of the Blue Room and she made sure that it was historically authentic to the period of James Monroe. She did the same with the Map Room and made it look how it looked during World War II.

She worked with interior decorator Kaki Hockersmith and in the period that she was a first lady she made numerous changes and redecorations around the building making it look brighter. She hosted many events at the White House some of which were more famous such as the state dinner for visiting Chinese dignitaries, the New Year's Eve celebration at the turn of the 21st century, and the state dinner honoring the bicentennial of the White House in November of 2000.

Hilary founded and initiated Save America's Treasures, for preserving and restoring historic items and sites and it was funded by federal funds and private donations. She was the head of the White House Millennium Council and the hostess of the Millennium Evenings which were a series of lectures that deliberated future studies. She created the first White House Sculpture Garden that was located in the Jacqueline Kennedy Garden which displayed a lot of art loaned from museums.

Michelle Obama

Michelle Obama became the First Lady in 2009 when Barack Obama was elected as a President of the United States. Michelle visited homeless shelters and soup kitchens during the first months as a First Lady. She advocated public service and sent representatives to schools. In celebration for the enactment of the Lilly Ledbetter Fair Pay Act of 2009 pay equality law, she hosted a reception at the White House to offer her support for women's rights. Some of the critics thought that she should be less involved in politics while others thought that she was very good at what she did.

In 2009, on 5 June it was announced from the White House that Michelle Obama will be replacing the current chief of staff Jackie Norris with Susan Sher who was a good friend of hers and adviser. That same year, Michelle

Obama was named Most Fascinating Person of the year by Barbara Walters.

She took many initiatives as a First Lady, and some of them include advocating on behalf of military families, encouraging national service, helping women balance their career and family and promoting education about art. She especially made a big deal out of supporting the spouses of military men and women and her personal mission has been bonding with those families.

She is very emotionally involved in stories of the sacrifice that military people make for their country. Barack and Michelle were awarded the Jerald Washington memorial Founders' Award in April 2012 by the National Coalition for Homeless Veterans. This award is the highest honor that can be given to people that advocate for veterans. Obama was once more awarded this honor in May 2015. Michelle was also one of the first people in the administration that pointed out obesity as a rising problem in the U.S. She advocated a solution through promoting healthy eating habits and leading a healthier life overall.

In May 2014, Michelle joined the campaign for bringing school girls back who had been kidnapped in Nigeria. She tweeted a picture of herself holding a poster with a hashtag that said #bringbackourgirls. Over the entire presidency of Barack Obama, there were a lot of speculations about whether Michelle should run for president herself.

In 2009 CNN did a poll asking whether the people thought that she should run for president in 2020 and 83% of the people who answered the poll were opposed to the idea. During a meeting, Barack was asked if the possibility of Michelle running for president is on the table. He dismissed that possibility. On another occasion he again denied that she would ever want to do that, giving a reason that she wants to impact as many people as possible in an unbiased way.

Michelle promoted healthy eating by planting the White House Kitchen Garden which is an organic garden and the first White House vegetable garden since Eleanor Roosevelt. She also installed bee hives on the South Lawn at the White House. The garden produced organic foods and honey that the First Family consumed along with guests of state dinners and official events.

"Let's Move!" was an initiative created by Michelle Obama in January 2010. With this initiative, Michelle wanted to reverse the 21st-century trend of childhood obesity. After presenting the initiative, Barack Obama created the Task Force on Childhood Obesity in order to review the problem and to create a nationwide plan about addressing this rising problem. Michelle said that her goal was to leave something as her legacy, to promote positive changes and to leave a footprint in the world's history.

She thought that childhood obesity was a great place where changes were necessary. In 2012 she released a book named American Grown: The Story of the White House Kitchen Garden and Gardens across America which was based on her experience with the garden that she initiated and its purpose was to promote healthy eating habits. The United States Department of Defense supported her. A lot of opposing parties criticized and ridiculed Michelle's efforts to promote healthy eating.

In May 2009, Obama visited UC Merced in Merced County, California at their graduating ceremony and delivered a speech. The students loved her and Kevin Fagan of the San Francisco Chronicle wrote that there was chemistry between Michelle and the students at the UC Merced. In August 2013 Obama was a guest at the 50th-anniversary ceremony for the March on Washington that was being held at the Lincoln Memorial. Her attire which was designed by Tracy Reese which brought her a lot of positive attention. In March 2015 she traveled to Selma, Alabama along with her family to honor the 50th anniversary of the Selma to Montgomery marches.

That same year in July, Michelle went to Coachella and Los Angeles for the Special Olympics World Games. Later, in October, together with Prince Harry and Jill Biden, they visited a military base in Fort Belvoir, Virginia. This visit was an effort by the prince to raise awareness to programs that are supporting armed service members. In December 2015, Barack and Michelle visited San Bernardino in California to support the families of the victims of a terrorist attacks that occurred there two weeks earlier.

Thanks for Reading

Hello, this message is from Naven Johnson. I hope that you enjoyed this book and that it has helped your life in some way. It is my intention to create information that readers will find useful and valuable.

I am grateful when people read books and I are even more grateful when my readers leave a review. Please leave a review that lets me know what you liked about this book so that I can work on improving future books.